A Little Book About the Greatest Book

The Greatest Book Ever!

Teresa Joyelle Krager

illustrated by Jesús Lopez

B&H kids
Brentwood TN

Dedication:
To Briana and Joshua,
May God's Word delight your heart
as you delight in Him. (Psalm 37:4)
With all my love ~ Mom

Text copyright © 2023 by Teresa Joyelle Krager
Art copyright © 2023 by B&H Publishing Group
Published by B&H Publishing Group, Brentwood, Tennessee
All rights reserved.
978-1-0877-6981-3
Dewey Decimal Classification: C220.95
Subject Heading: BIBLE \ BIBLE—READING \ BIBLE STORIES
Printed in Shenzhen, Guangdong, China, March 2023
1 2 3 4 5 6 · 27 26 25 24 23

You may be surprised,
But this is a book
That points to another.
You must take a look

At a book called the Bible—
Words whispered by God!
Come hear favorite highlights.
Feel free to applaud.

Let's start with creation.
How did God do it?
He spoke, and His Word
Made the world! Nothing to it.

First light, day and night,
Waving seas and dry land,
Creatures of all kinds,
Then woman and man.

4

Our world's big beginning—
How do we know?
God says in the Bible.
That means it is so.

God gave Noah plans
For a large floating zoo.
This ark saved his family
And animals too.

Jonah tried running
Away from God's reach,
Spent three days in a fish,
Got spit out on a beach!

God helped some be bold.
Moses split the Red Sea.

Deborah saw Israel's
Enemies flee.

Rahab—the spy keeper,
Joshua—the scout,

10

Watched city walls fall
When men gave a loud *shout*.

Learn of brave Daniel.
Was he lion dinner?

Gideon outnumbered—
His army, the winner!

Elijah flew up
In a chariot of fire!

Elisha crossed Jordan—
The riverbed drier.

A boy killed a giant
With slingshot and stone.

One king was age seven
When he took the throne.

While keeping her secret,
A girl was crowned queen,
Then risked her own life
In a grand throne room scene.

Yes, God helped these heroes.
We named just a few
Of the Bible adventures
Where stories are true.

God spoke to people
Through angels and fire,
A voice from a cloud,
The song of a choir,

A whisper, the wind,
A vision or dream.
God shared hidden secrets
No others had seen!

And then . . . silence.
No message was heard.
For four hundred years—
Nothing new, not a word.

Until suddenly . . .

Angels announced
That God's Son came to earth!

You can learn about Jesus,
The day of His birth.

He grew up and worked wonders.
Great stories, He told.
If all written down,
The whole world could not hold.

Jesus walked on the water
As if it were land,

Healed the sick, raised the dead,
Made the paralyzed stand.

He stopped a fierce storm,

And five thousand were fed

From one boy's sack lunch
Of two fish and five bread.

Jesus loved everyone,
All He created—
Even the friendless,
The ones sometimes hated.

When moms brought their children
For Jesus to touch,
He said, "Let them come."
Yes, He loved them that much.

Jesus *is* love
And Jesus loves *you!*
His book's a love letter,
Trustworthy and true.

Read how God's Son
Died for everyone's sin.
Men, women, and children,
All heroes need Him.

Jesus came to our rescue!
Our hands will applaud.
He rose back to life,
Is in heaven with God.

Jesus said He'll return.
He announced, "Watch and see.
I'll come back for all people
Believing in Me,

Who say they are sorry
For wrongs they have done
And receive God's forgiveness,
A gift from the Son."

You'll want to read more
Because you've only heard
A quick teasing of tidbits
Of truths from God's Word.

The rest of each story
You'll find in *His* book—
The greatest book ever.
Go, take a look!

The revelation of your words brings light
and gives understanding to the inexperienced.

(Psalm 119:130 CSB)

COME, TAKE A LOOK!

The Bible is also called God's Word, Scripture, and the Holy Bible. To learn more about a story mentioned in this little book, look up the book, chapter, and verse(s) in the Bible using this chart.

Page	Event or Fact	Scripture Reference(s)
3	Words whispered by God	2 Timothy 3:16
4–5	The beginning (creation)	Genesis 1
6	Noah's ark	Genesis 6:9–7:16
7	Jonah in the big fish	Jonah 1:17–2:10
8	Moses split the Red Sea	Exodus 14:5–31
9	Deborah led Israel's army	Judges 4:4–16
10	Rahab hid Joshua's spies	Joshua 2; 6:25
10	Joshua scouted the land	Numbers 13:16–25
11	Fall of Jericho's walls	Joshua 6:1–20
12	Daniel in the lion's den	Daniel 6:6–23
12	Gideon with his small army	Judges 7:1–22
13	Elijah's ride to heaven	2 Kings 2:1–12
13	Elisha crossed the Jordan River	2 Kings 2:13–14
14	David killed a giant	1 Samuel 17:17–50
14	Seven-year-old king	2 Kings 11:1–12, 18–21
15	Esther crowned queen	Esther 2:1–17
15	Esther risked her life	Esther 4:11–5:2
15	God helped His people	Psalm 118:7; Hebrews 13:6
	God spoke through:	
16	– Angels	Genesis 16:7–9; Luke 1:26–38
16	– Fire	Exodus 3:1–5
16	– Cloud	Exodus 19:16–19
16	– Choir	Luke 2:13–14
16	– Whisper	1 Kings 19:12–13
16	– Wind	Job 38:1
16	– Vision	Genesis 15:1; Daniel 2:19; Revelation 9:17
16	– Dream	Matthew 2:13, 19, and 22

Page	Event or Fact	Scripture Reference(s)
18	Angels told of Jesus's birth	Luke 1:26–33; 2:10–12; Matthew 1:18–21
18	Jesus's birth (Christmas)	Luke 2:1–20
19	Jesus grew	Luke 2:41–52
19	Examples of Jesus's teachings	Matthew 5–7, 13, 18, 20, 24, 25
19	Not enough room for the writings of Jesus's ministry	John 21:25
	Examples of Jesus's miracles:	
20	– Jesus walked on water	Matthew 14:22–33; Mark 6:45–51; John 6:16–21
20	– Jesus healed the sick	Luke 4:38–39; 5:12–13; 7:1–10; 8:27–36
20	– Jesus raised the dead	Mark 5:22–24; 38–42; Luke 7:11–15; John 11:38–44
20	– The paralyzed walked	Matthew 9:2–7; Mark 2:3–12; Luke 5:18–25
21	– A storm was calmed	Matthew 8:23–27; Mark 4:37–41; Luke 8:22–25
21	– Five thousand people fed	Matthew 14:15–21; Mark 6:30–44; Luke 9:12–17; John 6:5–13
22	Jesus loved everyone	Luke 15:11–32 (rebellious son); Mark 2:13–17 (tax collector); Mark 12:41–44 (poor widow); Mark 14:3–9 (woman who anointed Jesus); John 8:1–11 (woman caught in adultery)
22	Children come to Jesus	Matthew 19:13–15; Mark 10:13–16; Luke 18:15–17
23	Jesus/God is love	1 John 4:8, 16
23	Jesus/God loves you	John 3:16; 1 John 4:9–11
23	The Bible is trustworthy and true	2 Samuel 7:28; Psalm 119:160; Hebrews 6:18; Revelation 21:5
24	Jesus is the Son of God	Matthew 16:13–17; Romans 1:1–4
24	Jesus died for our sin	John 1:29; Matthew 27:45–54; 1 Peter 3:18
25	Jesus came to our rescue	Galatians 1:3–4
25	Jesus rose back to life	Matthew 28:1–7; Mark 16:1–6; Luke 24:1–8; John 20:1–8
25	Jesus is in heaven with God	Acts 7:55; Romans 8:34; Hebrews 1:3
26	Jesus promised to return	Matthew 16:27; Mark 13:26–27; Acts 1:11
26–27	Belief and confession	John 3:16–17; 20:31; Romans 10:9–10
27	Forgiveness of sin	Acts 10:43; 13:38; Ephesians 1:7; Colossians 1:13–14
27	Salvation is God's gift	Romans 6:23; Ephesians 2:8

REMEMBER

"He showed you these things so you would know that the LORD is God and there is no other."
(Deuteronomy 4:35 NLT)

READ

Most Bible heroes were ordinary people who simply believed that God was who He said He was and obeyed when He called them. Look back through *The Greatest Book Ever!* and find some of the difficult tasks God asked people to do. Turn to the "Come, Take a Look!" table on pages 30–31. Pick a topic you would like to hear more about and read its Bible reference(s). Discuss some of the new details you learned and something that surprised you.

THINK

1. Name some of your favorite Bible heroes and why you like them.

2. What were some ways God helped His people in troubling situations?

3. How often do you take time to read or listen to the Bible? How does it change how you think, feel, or act?

4. What is something God might call you to do? How will you respond?